KU-332-484
MILWAUKEE ROAD
SOUTHERN PACIFIC
WABASH
MILWAUKEE
MILWAUKEE ROAD
MILWAUKEE ROAD
GREAT NORTHERN
MILW
MILWAUKEE
N&W
NORFOLK AND WESTERN
NEW YORK CENTRAL SYSTEM
L&N
LOUISVILLE & NASHVILLE
FRISCO
SL-SF
19686
SOUTHEAST... SOUTHWEST
Ship it on the Frisco!

TRAINS

BY JOHN WESTWOOD

Galley Press

CONTENTS

Title page: The star of the film *Murder on the Orient Express*, No. 230.G.353, a preserved 4–6–0 of the former Paris–Orléans railway.
This page: Although once regularly used on the Union Pacific Railroad's transcontinental passenger services, No. 8444 is now preserved for use on special trains.

INTRODUCTION

'At one time the passengers by the engine had the pleasure of accompanying and cheering their brother passengers by the stage coach, which passed alongside, and of observing the striking contrast exhibited by the power of the engine and of horses; the engine with her six hundred passengers and load, and the coach with four horses, and only sixteen passengers.'

That perceptive observer, writing of the opening day of the Stockton & Darlington Railway in the north-east of England on 27 September 1825, had grasped – though he may not have realized it – the essential change that made railways perhaps the most revolutionary means of transport since the invention of the wheel. Horsepower was slow and expensive (footpower, and the vast majority could not afford horses, was even slower); engine-power was faster, and trains more comfortable and reliable, and ran more frequently and carried more passengers (and more freight), than stage-coaches.

On that day George Stephenson's engine *Locomotion* travelled at a regular speed of 19km/h (12mph), sometimes reaching as much as 24km/h (15mph). The inaugural trip on the world's first public railway to be worked by a steam locomotive had been run.

Despite the cheering crowds and the bands, railways were not a new invention. They did not spring fully fledged from the inventive brain of George Stephenson, supported by the pockets of the directors of the Stockton & Darlington. Stationary steam engines had been used in mines for over a century and railways had been employed in industrial districts for longer than that. The trains consisted of trucks running on rails made of wood or iron, and pulled by a horse. They took coal and minerals from the quarries and mines to the canals and the coast.

In England in the early nineteenth century – stimulated by, and in turn stimulating, the demands of the burgeoning industrial revolution – these two trends came together. In 1804 the Cornish engineer Richard Trevithick built an engine that pulled five wagons, loaded with passengers and iron ore, on a private line in South Wales: the track broke under its weight. Four years later, he took another model to London and set it up not far from where Euston station, one of the capital's main-line termini, was later built. Thousands rode on it. George Stephenson took over where Trevithick left off and spent several years improving locomotive design. In 1821 he was appointed engineer to the Stockton & Darlington. The interesting thing about Stephenson's railway was that it was by no means certain that locomotives would be used. The directors had originally planned to use horses, and until 1833 horses pulled the passenger trains, and locomotives the freight. Nor had they originally planned a regular timetable.

So, the hullabaloo notwithstanding, 27 September 1825 hardly started the railway age at all, and the Stockton & Darlington is better remembered as one stage in the developing story of railways. If the beginning of the railway age has to be marked by one single event, that honour goes without question to the Liverpool & Manchester Railway. George Stephenson's *Rocket* won the trials held to determine the most suitable engine for the trains. The railway was a huge success; in its first year it carried 460,000 passengers (less than a quarter of that number had made the journey by stagecoach the previous year) and brought the cities within two hours of one another.

The early chapters of the railway story are predominantly British but the first lines in many countries were not far behind the Liverpool & Manchester – only four months in the USA, where the South Carolina Railroad began operations in January 1831 – and by the end of the 1830s there

On the right is one of the famous French compound locomotives of the Nord Railway.

NORD
3142

were lines in France, Ireland, Canada, Germany, Russia, Holland, Belgium, Italy and the Austro-Hungarian Empire.

Historians debate at length about the relationship between railways, the industrial revolution and the growth of towns. What can definitely be said is that railways helped to break down the localized nature of society and of the economy. Before the railways, people simply did not travel very much; the vast majority spent their entire lives where they had been born. Railways helped personal mobility and brought more and more people to the expanding cities. Before the railways, too, such industry as there was had to be sited near the raw materials it used; a sizeable railway network meant that raw materials could be sent wherever they were needed.

Agriculture changed too. Traditionally, local communities had grown most of the food they consumed themselves; railways meant that food could be distributed throughout the nation, especially after refrigerated cars were introduced. In the United States, cattle no longer had to be driven hundreds, perhaps thousands, of miles to the Chicago stockyards but were simply loaded on to trains at the nearest railhead.

In other ways, too, the railways helped to unify individual nations. Mail distribution speeded up enormously. Newspapers could now be delivered hundreds of miles overnight, so their circulation increased, their price decreased, and more people could feel more in touch with one another.

The first excursion was organized in 1840, and later thousands and then millions came to take an annual holiday by train. And, from the last decades of the nineteenth century onwards, in a process that continues today, the construction of underground railways and suburban lines made travelling within major cities easier and encouraged the growth of suburbs, easily reached after a day's work in the centre.

As more and more railways were built, so the services they provided became increasingly sophisticated. The first passenger cars were primitive, and on the earliest lines third-class passengers might travel in freight cars. They soon became more comfortable, especially after bogies (fitted beneath each coach to ease it round curves) were introduced. Pullman cars (named after their American inventor, George Pullman) first ran in 1859 and dining-cars and sleeping-cars appeared in 1867. In the 1930s, observation cars were the

fashion, especially on transcontinental journeys. Nowadays, travellers in some countries expect air-conditioning, loudspeaker announcements and, on the crack Trans-Europe Expresses for instance, a telephone and secretarial services.

There have been similar improvements in safety. Continuous and automatic braking systems were important steps forward. In signalling, the biggest advance came when the block system was made compulsory. This divides the track into blocks; only one train may be in a block at any time. Semaphore signals by the side of the track and controlled from a signal box had already replaced a system of flags, boards and discs, themselves preceded by hand signals given by signalmen – originally known as policemen – standing at the side of the track. Semaphore signals have now by and large given way to coloured-light signals, and the traditional trackside signal boxes have been transformed into computerized control centres from which one signalman can control a hundred-mile stretch of line. Additional automatic safety checks have also been developed.

The biggest change of all, of course, has been in locomotives. Stephenson's *Rocket* is but a distant relation of the streamlined *Mallard*, which reached 203km/h (126mph) in 1938, setting a world record, and of the gigantic American *Big Boys* of the 1940s, which weighed over 400 tons. But the steam engine was inefficient and wasted most of the energy contained in coal; it needed considerable maintenance and was hard on the permanent way. Electric and then diesel locomotives began to be developed towards the end of the nineteenth century and slowly came into service in the first decades of the twentieth. It was virtually inevitable that sooner or later they would replace steam. That in fact did not happen on a large scale until after World War II but once they prevailed, higher speeds, greater power and more intensive use offset the greater cost of the locomotives and, in the case of electricity, of installing trackside equipment.

Despite the competition from cars – which make local journeys far more convenient – and from aircraft – which make long-distance travel far quicker – railways seem to be holding their own.

Left: A Union Pacific Railroad diesel-electric road-switcher at work on a branch line in Idaho. *Below:* The interior of a steam locomotive cab, with its array of gauges and valves.

165
165

STEAM

Scenes like this, showing a middle-aged Pacific of the Milwaukee Railroad hauling a local passenger train out of Chicago, disappeared in the mid 1950s. However, as the following pages show, steam has not yet disappeared from all the world's railways.

Great Britain

The Great Western Railway in England was a great user of the 2–6–2 tank locomotive, both for its city commuter services and for its branch lines. The 4500 class, illustrated below, was one of the earliest designs, being introduced in the early years of this century. With a pair of guiding wheels at each end, the 2–6–2 could run fast in both directions, making it ideal for short-distance passenger services where there was no opportunity to use a turntable at the end of each run. This particular locomotive, No. 4555, is now preserved, and is used on the Dart Valley Railway in Devon, a railway that was once a Great Western branch line.

Also of the 2–6–2 wheel arrangement, but of very different form and function, was the *Green Arrow* (*right*) of the London & North Eastern Railway. Designed originally for fast freight services in the 1930s, it was also widely used on passenger services. During World War II locomotives of this type hauled passenger trains of up to 24 vehicles, which were unprecedented loads for British railways. Designed by Nigel Gresley, it resembled his other designs in its boiler. This boiler enabled high power outputs to be maintained for long distances, and also necessitated the short chimney carried by the *Green Arrows*. Clearances on British lines could not accommodate both a wide-diameter boiler and a normal chimney. The resemblance to the *Flying Scotsman* (see page 14) is striking, and the type may be regarded as a scaled-down version of that locomotive.

GREEN ARROW
L N E R
4771

GREAT WESTERN

In Britain, the usual wheel arrangement for heavy freight locomotives was 2–8–0. The eight driving wheels provided good tractive qualities while the leading pair of smaller wheels helped ease the locomotive round curves. One of the most successful examples of this type was the class 8F of the London, Midland & Scottish Railway. Several hundred units were built, and some were sent to the Middle East for war service. A handful are still in existence on the Turkish railways. No. 8233, illustrated here, has been preserved, and is shown hauling a train on the Severn Valley Railway. William Stanier, who designed these locomotives, originally worked for the Great Western Railway, and his designs had certain GWR features, like the sharply tapered boiler and generally gaunt appearance.

The pride of the Great Western Railway's locomotive department were the thirty 'King' class locomotives (*above right*). Of the 4–6–0 wheel arrangement, and with four cylinders, they were the final development of the 4-cylinder 4–6–0 introduced by the GWR in the first

decade of this century. First had come the 'Stars', then the famous 'Castles', and then in the late 1920s the 'Kings', which were simply an enlarged 'Castle'. Unfortunately, lineside clearances were inadequate for anything larger than the 'Kings', and the latter remained the Great Western Railway's most powerful passenger locomotive. No. 6000, *King George V*, is one of two members of the class that have been preserved. Owned by a cider company, it makes frequent appearances on special trains. Early in its career it visited the USA, after which it carried an American locomotive bell.

At the end of the 1970s the only regular steam operations in Britain, apart from the tourist and preserved services, were the coal trains of the National Coal Board. A few collieries still used steam locomotives for these, most commonly of the design illustrated left. These 0–6–0 saddle-tank engines are of a design built in large numbers for use by the British Army in World War II. This particular example has been modernized with the Austrian *Giesl* exhaust, recognizable by its distinctive chimney.

Already celebrated in the 1920s, No. 4472 *Flying Scotsman* (*right*) is now one of the world's best-known preserved locomotives. Built originally to haul the London to Edinburgh trains of the London & North Eastern Railway, the class broke several speed records and remained in service right up to the end of steam traction.

One of several A4 class locomotives that are now preserved, the No. 4498 (*far right*) was named in honour of its designer, Sir Nigel Gresley. It is one of this type, *Mallard*, which holds the official world speed record for steam traction.

Below is another view of the Great Western Railway's *King George V*. The widely different design philosophies of the GWR and the LNER companies are well illustrated by the pictures on these two pages.

L N E R
4498
SIR NIGEL GRESLEY

6000
BRITISH RAILWAYS

SOUTHERN
ATLANTIC
COAST EXPRESS

Although Britain's Southern Railway was largely electrified, it did introduce a distinctive range of steam locomotives (*left*). This culminated in the 4–6–2 locomotives designed by Oliver Bulleid, one of the most innovative of locomotive designers. These had an outer covering (termed air-smoothing, not streamlining), one of whose purposes was to make the locomotives suitable for passing through mechanical washing installations. Other features were American-style disc driving wheels, valve gear driven by chains instead of rods, and a large boiler tapered at the bottom. The first series were the 30 units of the 'Merchant Navy' class. These were intended for fast, heavy passenger trains, but because they appeared in World War II, when it was considered that purely passenger locomotives were an unjustified luxury, they were described as 'mixed traffic'. After Bulleid's departure his successors rebuilt most of these locomotives, removing the air-smoothing and the chain-driven valve gear. The locomotive illustrated, No. 21C 123 *Blackmore Vale*, is an unrebuilt example of the 'West Country' class. It is shown here at work on the Bluebell Railway, where it is now preserved. It is carrying the headboards of the 'Atlantic Coast Express', the Southern Railway's most prestigious train, which ran from London to the Cornish seaside resorts.

A complete contrast in railway preservation (*above*) is a scene on the narrow gauge Talyllyn Railway in Wales.

Continental Europe

Relatively few French steam locomotives have been preserved in working order. In fact, two of the most outstanding French designs are represented outside France, in England. One of these is an example of the earlier, compound locomotives. The other is a later development, a 4–6–2 originally built by the Paris–Orléans Railway and later rebuilt according to the principles of the celebrated locomotive engineer André Chapelon. Chapelon's improvements included the use of high-temperature steam, a double-bore chimney designed to exert a steady draught on the fire without drawing excessive amounts of unburned fuel from the grate, and a smoothing of internal steam passages. The latter measure, by streamlining the pipes through which the steam passed, conserved the energy contained in the latter. Over the years, many older classes of locomotive received the Chapelon treatment, which gave an increased power output for lesser expenditure of fuel and water. In general, the French passenger compound locomotive could be regarded as the most sophisticated breed of steam traction in the world, but it relied largely on the knowledge and skill of its crews. French locomotive crews were more highly trained than those of other countries, needing to handle the more complex controls of a compound engine and to handle minor repairs and adjustments. It would have been unsuitable for American conditions, where robust engines were required, capable of enduring the rough-and-ready life of US railroad operation. In Britain, where coal was cheap, the fuel economy of the French locomotive was more than balanced by its greater maintenance expenses. The locomotive top left is of the 231K class, and is preserved at Steamtown, Carnforth, Lancashire, England.

The 2–6–0 of the former Est Railway of France (*right*) is not of a well-known class, but nevertheless has many features of the typical French locomotive of the turn of the century.

Another French preserved line is the metre-gauge Vivarais line (*top right*), a former 'line of local significance' now operated by enthusiasts.

403
FACS

744 015

Although a pioneer and innovator in electric traction, Italy produced few notable steam locomotives. Such inventiveness as there was was largely devoted to the design of devices to reduce fuel consumption as Italy is devoid of coal and oil resources. The locomotive illustrated (*far left*) is a typical example of the power used by the Italian State Railways in the final decades of steam operation. It is a 2–8–0 of the 744 class, intended for freight service but capable of hauling the slower passenger trains. By the end of the 1970s, steam traction in Italy was confined to a few shunting and short transfer workings, although a considerable number of steam locomotives were retained for emergency use.

In Portugal at the end of the 1970s steam traction could still be found on the narrow gauge but scenes such as the one on the left, showing a 4–6–0 on the broad gauge, had disappeared. Below is an interesting line-up of power on the broad gauge Spanish National Railways. In the centre is a diesel locomotive, representative of a type now responsible for all work on the non-electrified lines. On the left is a working replica of a locomotive dating from the earliest years of Spanish railways.

With East Germany, Austria may now be regarded as the last home of the European narrow-gauge steam railway (*below*). Several lines, widely distributed, are still in operation, serving the daily needs of their localities as well as an increasing number of tourists. One of the busiest and best-known of such lines, and one of several owned and operated by the Austrian State Railways, is that which once ran from Garsten to Klaus but which has recently been shortened. Tank locomotives of the standard 298 class are used on this line, handling both freight and passenger services. The most common gauge is 76cm (2ft 6in) and several of these narrow-gauge lines, nominally dieselized, have found it worthwhile to retain their old steam locomotives for tourist trains.

In Switzerland, thanks to abundant hydro-electricity, the steam locomotive began to disappear quite early, even though there was a well-established steam locomotive industry supplying both the home and overseas market. (Swiss locomotives can still be seen at work in Indonesia.) However, the metre-gauge Rhaetian Railway, one of the largest of the railways not coming within the Swiss National Railways system, retains a pair of 2–8–0 locomotives (*right*) for use on special trains. The fine mountain scenery of the Engadine district is an additional attraction for the public, but it also means that the line is heavily graded; the use of two locomotives is not to gratify the sightseer, but to meet operating requirements.

Rh.B. 107

Following the formation of the German State Railways (DR) from the old railway systems after World War I, a new range of standard locomotives was designed and built. Based largely on the practice of the Prussian State Railways, the largest of the former systems, locomotives were intended to be cheap to maintain above all else. High power output was a secondary consideration. The most numerous of the new locomotives was the 2-cylinder freight design, which appeared in several variations. In its lightweight version, it was adopted as the standard war locomotive, and thousands of these *Kriegsloks* served not only in Germany, but in the countries occupied by Germany. After the war many hundreds of these machines were retained by the newly liberated countries, and some are still at work in Poland and Roumania. Above is a front view of one of these locomotives which until recently worked in West Germany and (*right*) another of the class at work in the same country.

050 281-5

424.075

556 0506

Eastern Europe

Some remarkable locomotive types were built in the countries of Central Europe between the wars. Notable among these was the type 424 4–8–0 built initially for the Hungarian State Railways but later exported to Yugoslavia, North Korea, and (involuntarily after the war) to the USSR. Intended for both passenger and freight service, it proved robust and fast. The picture (*left*) shows one of the class on a secondary passenger train consisting of four-wheel vehicles. It is on such trains that the majority of the class are now employed.
Another view of the Hungarian 424 class, showing the unusual height of the boiler above the frames, is below. The first examples of the class appeared in the 1920s, but at that time machines of such power were not really needed. However, in World War II the design justified itself, and about 500 units were built. The wide chimney and smoke deflectors are a later addition.
After World War II Czech locomotive design was strongly influenced by the French, as can be seen in the picture (*below left*) of a 556 class 2–10–0, photographed at Gmünd (Austria) on a cross-frontier service.

North America

In the USA the most successful preserved railways have been those whose main appeal has been directed towards the family sightseer. In the Rocky Mountains of Colorado the narrow gauge network that was once a flourishing part of the Denver and Rio Grande Railroad has long been abandoned, but two sections are still used for tourist steam trains. One of these is the celebrated and successful Silverton line, still operated by the D & RGW with the original locomotives. The other (*below*) is the 103km (64m) Cumbres and Toltec Railroad, which is aided by the States of Colorado and New Mexico. This also uses the original 2–8–2 3ft gauge motive power, as shown.

One of the most successful tourist lines is the Strasburg Railroad in the heart of Pennsylvania's scenic and quaint 'Dutch Country' (*right*). Built originally in 1832, and therefore a claimant to the title of America's oldest short line, this 7.2-km (4.5-mile) property was purchased by a group of businessmen in 1958, by which time its freight traffic had dwindled to little more than a carload per day. Having discovered that a restored passenger service might produce far more revenue than freight, the new owners introduced a passenger service intended to recreate the atmosphere of the 19th-century short line. About 9,000 passengers were carried in 1959, and this rose to about 400,000 over the next two decades. This prosperity has made it possible to purchase genuine 19th-century buildings and to create workshops capable of handling heavy locomotive repairs, as well as to acquire a carefully selected stock of locomotives. No. 89 (*right*) is an 0–6–0 that once belonged to the Canadian National Railways and probably never hauled a passenger train until it arrived on the Strasburg Railroad, since it was designed for yard work. This locomotive did most of the work in the early years, and is still well-used.

A later addition to the Strasburg Railroad's stock was No. 1223 (*below right*), once a fast passenger locomotive of the neighbouring Pennsylvania Railroad. This locomotive is a very typical machine of the late 19th-century US railroad, since it has the 4–4–0, or 'American', wheel arrangement.

CARPENTERS
89

1223
STRASBURG RAIL ROAD

1533
NEW HOPE & IVYLAND

Another steam tourist line which was offering weekend trips in the 1970s was the New Hope and Ivyland Railroad in Pennsylvania. Perhaps in an attempt to differentiate itself from other such lines, this railroad went a step closer to real-life short-line operation by operating not a passenger train, but a mixed train. Such trains were very common in America during the steam era, not only on short lines but also on the branches of the big railroad companies. A mixed train, typically, was a freight train which peddled freight cars at each station and included, at the tail end, a passenger car. On the New Hope and Ivyland the train consisted of a coach and caboose, the latter being able to accommodate any small items of freight that might be forthcoming. There was a weekly service, in the summer months, of a train leaving on Saturday evening and making the round trip in three-and-a-half hours. The fare was four dollars, with a one-dollar supplement for those wishing to ride in the caboose. The motive power was usually 4–6–0 No. 1533, pictured left. This locomotive originally belonged to the Canadian National Railways. Because the Canadian Pacific and the Canadian National were the last big North American railways to operate steam locomotives, they became a source of motive power for new tourist railways in the USA.

To survive, tourist and preserved lines in the USA needed to attract not just railway enthusiasts but the general public. This meant that sometimes 'attractions' had to be offered which might conflict with the authenticity of the preservation. Such attractions might have included, in extreme cases, Red Indian attacks. More typically, they involved the painting of rolling stock in fancy colours (*below*).

484
484
KEEP
OFF
KEEP
OFF

6060
6060
DANGER
BI-LEVEL CARS
MUST NOT ENTER

Like most 3ft, 3ft 6in and metre gauge locomotives, the 484 is hardly a true narrow gauge machine. It is no smaller than a standard gauge locomotive, only the width between the wheels is less. The close-up (*above*) shows additional details. The powerful pump and long piping is characteristic of American steam locomotives, and is connected to the Westinghouse compressed air brake standard in the USA. The leading dome is for sand, this being the favoured position for sand supplies (in contrast to British locomotives, which carried it beneath the running board). The short but sharp taper of the boiler is also typically American. However, the outside cranks and counterweights are a feature not of American practice but of the narrower gauges, where internal clearances are too small to accommodate these parts between the frames. The bell, actuated by a cord from the cab, is for warning pedestrians and vehicles at road crossings; road bridges were relatively rare in the USA, even in towns. More modern locomotives had bells actuated mechanically, freeing the crew for other duties.

After the Canadian National Railways completed their dieselization programme they retained a heavy passenger steam locomotive for excursion service. Initially this was one of the CNR's celebrated Mountain, or 4–8–4, machines. The second locomotive was No. 6060, shown here. This was a survivor of a class built in the 1940s, the Canadian National's last steam passenger locomotive design.

South America

Apart from the spectacular standard gauge and diesel-operated state railway in Peru, there are two sizeable narrow-gauge lines that still use steam traction. One of these is the Huancayo–Huancavelica Railway, of 3ft gauge (*above*). This is one of those lines which for years has been described as awaiting imminent dieselization but which somehow manage to continue with their steam locomotives. In the case of this railway, considerable strengthening and renewal of track was said to be needed before diesel locomotives could be used effectively. A batch of diesel locomotives ordered for the line were for this reason re-gauged and sent to work at Callao docks. On an average day this line operates a pair of passenger trains and a pair of freight. German, American and British locomotives are used, the two German being the youngest, having been delivered in 1950 and 1951 from Henschel. However, most of the work is done by three US 2–6–0 locomotives, built by Baldwin in the 1920s. This picture shows one of the Baldwins at Huancayo.
Above right is another of the Huancayo–Huancavelica Railway's Baldwin 2–6–0s,

hauling the daily passenger train near Huancayo. Until recently the railways of Brazil were little explored by railway enthusiasts. But off the main lines, in remote and often roadless terrain, there survive steam-operated lines of local importance, often narrow gauge. One of these is the VCAO (*left*), based on Sao Joao del Rei, a 2ft 6in gauge branch line now operated by the Brazilian Federal Railways. The line has about 15 locomotives, all built by Baldwin in the USA and of which the youngest is 60 years old and the oldest 90. The picture (*left*) shows two examples of this elderly locomotive stock. No. 40 is a 4–6–0 built in 1912, and No. 66 is a 2–8–0 built in 1889. Despite their age, the locomotives are kept in fine condition, and in general the locomotives, rolling stock, and general operation remain a living example of the railway scene around the turn of the century. The line follows the Rio das Mortes, serving a succession of villages which are not linked by a continuous road. At one time it extended for more than 100 miles but has since been cut back to a western terminus at Aureliano Mourao. The eastern terminus is at Antonio Carlos, and en route the mainline station of Belo Horizonte is served. Passenger traffic, and a regular demand for freight service from a local cement factory, suggest that this railway may survive for some years yet.

Africa

The Beyer-Garratt locomotive (*right*) was a peculiarly British product, and was mainly to be found working in the British Commonwealth, notably in parts of Africa. The East African Railways, serving Kenya, Uganda, and Tanganyika, bought progressively larger versions of these locomotives, most of which have now been withdrawn. Locomotive No. 87, shown here, is preserved as a museum piece. Essentially, the Beyer-Garratt was a variety of flexible wheelbase locomotive, and its ability to curve itself around short-radius track is well demonstrated in the picture below. Herbert Garratt, a British locomotive engineer, worked on several colonial railways before 1914. He developed the concept which was intended to solve the problem of introducing powerful locomotives on railways whose track and bridges could not accept heavy concentrated weights, and whose track was too curved to take locomotives with a large number of driving axles. What he did was to use two conventional engine chassis, and to rest each end of the boiler, on pivots, on these. Thus, in terms of wheels and cylinders, his locomotive was the equivalent of two conventional units, and adequate steam could be supplied because the boiler, slung low, could be of large diameter. Moreover, the absence of machinery beneath the boiler meant that the grate could be deep, and well ventilated. The separation of weight into two widely spaced sets of wheels meant that the total engine weight would never be on one span of a bridge.

87
K U R
87

E A R
5934

The South African Railways obtained most of their locomotives from British builders, especially from the North British Locomotive Company of Glasgow. However, the chief mechanical engineers of the SAR exercised a quite close control over the designs. With some exceptions, like the import of condensing locomotives for use in the waterless Karroo, and a brief interest in Mallet-type machines, locomotive development was an organic process, with basic designs being enlarged and improved over the decades. The SAR's liking for the 4–8–2 wheel arrangement dates from the appointment of David Hendrie as its chief mechanical engineer in 1910. Hendrie's 15AR class (illustrated below) appeared in 1914. Hendrie's successor Colonel F. R. Collins resigned from the SAR having been criticized for doing little to improve on the work of his predecessor. A. G. Watson, who then held office from 1929 to 1936, enlarged the well-tried 4–8–2 concept by building the powerful class 15E. It was locomotives based on the latter design, plus Garratts and condenser locomotives, which after the end of World War II handled the heavier trains in South Africa.
Although Collins had failed to design a good heavy-duty locomotive, he did make his mark by enlisting the locomotive builder's help in producing a very well-thought-out branch line locomotive (*right*). The SAR operates several long branch lines, laid with light rail and sometimes including bridges unable to withstand heavy axle-loads. Since gradients were often difficult a powerful machine was required. Collins' solution was his class 19 4–8–2, with an axle-load of less than 13.7 tonnes (tons) This excellent design was developed over the years, but in 1949 its final version took the form of a 2–8–4, class 24. This had an axle-load of only 11.7 tonnes (tons). One of this class, unofficially named *City of George*, is on the right.

CITY OF
GEORGE

Asia

Until 1947 there were virtually two great British railway systems, that of the so-called 'home railways' and that of the Empire of India. The Indian system incorporated characteristic British features such as solid and rather expensive track and bridges, and locomotives which were Indianized versions of familiar British designs. Such Indianization involved side shutters for the cabs, for protection against the sun, large headlights and true 'cowcatchers' (because in India, unlike Britain, the lines were not fenced and collisions with livestock were quite frequent). At the end of the 1970s, therefore, India and Pakistan are still using large numbers of British steam locomotives. The recent picture below shows one of the commonest types, an 0–6–0. As in Britain, the six-wheeler was the favourite type for secondary freight and passenger services, despite its somewhat rough riding compared to the 2–6–0 wheel arrangement. No. 2472 is one of the type which was transferred to the Pakistan Railways in 1947. Although dieselization and electrification have made great strides in Pakistan over the last two decades, there is still scope for steam operation on secondary services.

Indeed, steam operation is almost certainly cheaper than diesel for these duties. This locomotive has been converted to oil burning, like most Pakistan Railway's steam units. After 1947 the coal which formerly was brought from Eastern India ceased to be available and Pakistan was without suitable sources of her own. One point demonstrated by this picture is that the broad gauge 1676mm (5ft 6in) proved of little advantage to the designers. The boiler in particular, is small in relation to the width of the locomotive, but was as big as was needed. In the early days of Indian railways the British insisted on a uniform, but broad, gauge. But by the end of the century the 1676mm (5ft 6in) standard had been supplemented by no fewer than three others. The narrowest was the 600mm (2ft) gauge (*above*), and the most celebrated of these was the Darjeeling–Himalaya line, which still winds its way up steep gradients and horse-shoe curves from the plains up to Darjeeling.

In the number of steam locomotives still at work, China surpasses India and is the world's greatest user of steam traction. Indeed, it is possible that steam locomotives are still being built there, and certainly steam traction will last well into the 21st century. In the 1950s China received a good deal of technical help from the Soviet Union, and consequently the outward appearance of rolling stock and locomotives is very Russian. The passenger vehicles shown in the picture above, for example, with their high and rather square cross-section and fluted steel sides, are almost identical with the standard Soviet vehicles built since World War II. The locomotive, a Pacific, cannot be so closely identified as a Soviet type, for the 4–6–2 wheel arrangement is not favoured in the USSR. Nevertheless, chimney and inscriptions apart, it would not look out of place in the USSR.

The 2–10–2 heavy freight locomotive of the Chinese railways (*right*) has been built in large numbers and is a direct derivation of the Russian LV class. The latter, reputedly a very efficient machine, was built in only small numbers in the USSR, being overtaken by

electrification and dieselization in 1956. Presumably drawings and perhaps presses were then transferred to China. However, the Soviet version had a device which could shift weight from the carrying wheels to the driving wheels when maximum power was required, and the Chinese unit appears to lack this.

After China, India, and South Africa, the country with the most working steam locomotives in the late 1970s was Indonesia. Most of these were in Java, but there were some in Sumatra also. With diesels used on the main lines, steam traction was confined largely to the branch lines, on which services were very irregular. Although timetables did exist in the minds of local railwaymen, they were not always adhered to, and trains were often cancelled for days. On some of the long mountainous branches of southern Java large Mallet type locomotives were used on quite light services. One of these Mallet-hauled mixed trains is shown above. No. CC5017 is a 2–6–6–0 of American design; in fact it is representative of the Mallet-type locomotives built in the USA in the first quarter of this century.

GREAT RAILWAY EVENTS

1803 The Surrey Iron Railway opened, the world's first public railway.
1806 The Oystermouth Railway at Swansea in South Wales opened, in the following year becoming the first railway to carry fare-paying passengers.

1812 Steam locomotives first used in regular commercial service, on the Middleton Colliery railway near Leeds.

1825 Opening of the Stockton & Darlington, the first public railway to use steam traction.
1827 First railway in Austrian Empire opened, from Budweiss (now in Czechoslovakia).
1828 Official opening of the St. Etienne to Andrézieux railway, the first in France.
1829 Delaware & Hudson Canal Company opens its gravity-worked coal line between Carbondale and Honesdale.

1830 Baltimore & Ohio Railroad opens its first section with horse traction, the first public railway in the USA.
1830 Liverpool & Manchester Railway opened using steam power throughout.
1830 First section of the St. Etienne to Lyons Railway opened, the first in France to use steam.
1831 South Carolina Railroad opened, the first in USA to use steam traction on a regular basis.
1833 Accident at a road crossing on the Leicester & Swannington Railway in England. This is said to be the origin of the locomotive whistle, which was fitted to avoid similar accidents.
1834 Ireland's first railway, from Dublin to Kingstown (Dun Laoghaire), opened.
1835 Brussels to Malines railway opened. This was the first railway in Belgium and the first in the world to be built as part of a government-planned system.
1835 Nuremberg to Fürth railway opened.
1836 Festiniog Railway opened in Wales, the world's first narrow gauge public railway.
1836 Canada's first steam railway opened between Laprairie and St Jean.
1837 Paris–St Germain Railway opened, a private venture which stimulated further railway construction in France.
1838 London & Birmingham Railway opened.
1839 Naples to Portici line opened, Italy's first railway.
1839 The Netherlands' first railway opened between Amsterdam and Haarlem.

1840 Harrison's 4–4–0 locomotive *Gowan and Marx* averages 16km/h (10mph) with a 432-ton train over the Philadelphia & Reading Railroad.
1841 2134mm (7ft) gauge Great Western Railway opened between London and Bristol.
1842 Meudon accident near Versailles, the first major railway disaster, with 53 deaths.
1844 The first railway in Switzerland opened between Basle and St Ludwig.
1848 Barcelona–Mataro line opened, Spain's first railway.
1848 Great Western Railway locomotive *Great Britain* with a 100-ton train covers 85 kilometres (53 miles) in 47 minutes.

1853 The Great Indian Peninsula Railway opens India's first railway, from Bombay to Thana.
1854 Australia's first steam railway opened between Port Melbourne and Flinders Street.
1856 John Saxby patents his system of interlocking signals and points (switches), the greatest advance towards accident-free operation.
1857 The first steel rails, laid by the Midland Railway in England.
1859 George Pullman's first sleeping car service begins, between Chicago and Bloomington.

1860 London & North Western Railway installs the first water troughs in North Wales, enabling the 'Irish Mail' locomotive to take water without stopping.
1863 First steam railway in New Zealand opens, between Christchurch and Ferrymead.
1863 London's Metropolitan Railway, the first underground railway in the world, opens its first section.
1868 The first Mallet-type articulated locomotive built in Belgium.
1869 America's first transcontinental railroad completed by the Union Pacific and Central Pacific companies.

1871 The Mont Cenis Tunnel, first of the great Alpine tunnels, opened.
1879 Electric locomotive of von Siemens operated at Berlin exhibition.
1879 Collapse of Tay Bridge in Scotland with 78 deaths.

1881 Opening of first public electric railway near Berlin.
1886 Canadian Pacific Railway opened to the Pacific.
1886 Severn Tunnel, then the world's longest at 7.011km (4.4m), opened for traffic.
1886 de Glehn and du Bousquet design the first of the classic French compound locomotives.

1890 Opening of the world's first electric underground railway, the City and South London.
1893 Record run of the 'Empire State Express' between New York and Buffalo. Locomotive No. 999 said to have reached 180km/h (112mph).
1895 Baltimore & Ohio Railroad opens first mainline electric service, on a short length of line through Baltimore.

1901 Wilhelm Schmidt of the Prussian State Railways successfully applies his firetube superheater to a locomotive. This is the most significant advance in locomotive technology since the Stephensons.
1906 Opening of Simplon Tunnel, the world's longest, in the Swiss Alps.

1913 Södermanland Railway in Sweden introduces a diesel-electric railcar, the first successful application of the diesel engine in railway traction.
1915 A triple collision at Quintinshill in Scotland is Britain's worst railway disaster.
1917 Trans-Australian Railway opened, linking Western Australia with the eastern states.
1917 The world's worst railway disaster occurs near Modane in Italy, when a troop train derailment leaves over 500 fatalities.

1923 British railway amalgamation completed, merging 123 companies into four large railways.

1929 Cascade Tunnel opened, at 12.542km (7.8m) the longest in North America.

1932 Trains begin to cross the new Sydney Harbour Bridge.
1936 The locomotive *Mallard* of the London & North Eastern Railway reaches 203km/h (126mph), the final speed record for a steam locomotive.
1939 A German diesel multiple-unit train reaches 133mph.

1941 The first of the *Big Boys*, articulated 4–8–8–4 locomotives, and the world's biggest, built for the Union Pacific Railroad.
1948 Britain's railways are nationalized.

1955 A French electric locomotive reaches 330km/h (205mph) on trials between Hendaye and Bordeaux, a world speed record for conventional traction.
1957 West European railway administrations cooperate to introduce the *Trans Europ Express* (TEE) service.

1964 Opening of the New Tokaido Line in Japan, between Tokyo and Osaka. This is the first of the high-speed railways.
1968 British Railways withdraws its last standard gauge steam locomotives.
1969 Containers move between Japan and Britain over the 'Trans Siberian Land Bridge'.

1970 Regauging makes possible the introduction of the 'Indian Pacific' passenger service between Sydney and Perth.
1971 Amtrak (National Railroad Passenger Corporation) takes over responsibility for most passenger services over US railroads.
1976 Conrail, a government agency, takes over the Penn-Central and other unprofitable railroads in the eastern states of the USA.
1976 The Tanzam Railway, linking landlocked Zambia with the sea at Dar-es-Salaam, opened. One of the biggest railway projects of this century, it was built with Chinese assistance, and is 1,858.7km (1,155m) long.
1976 British Rail introduces High Speed Trains (HST) between London/Bristol/South Wales.

FERROCARRIL CHIHUAHUA AL PACIFICO

DIESEL AND ELECTRIC TRAINS

Although the aesthetic appeal of the steam locomotive is unsurpassable, the belief that electric and diesel traction is uniform and uninteresting is quite unfounded. This picture shows an American-built diesel locomotive. The railway is the Chihuahua Pacific, and the train has stopped to allow its passengers to enjoy the view at the line's highest point at 2690m (8825ft).

Europe

After World War II French industry and French Railways (*below*) took the lead in electrification. This lead lasted until the late 1970s, when it was challenged by the sophisticated locomotives produced by Swedish industry. A landmark in the 1950s was the progressive electrification southwards from Paris to Marseilles. The extra traffic attracted to this line by electrification was an encouragement to both French and overseas railway administrations to electrify further. The low-voltage direct current system used on the Marseilles line was superseded by the technically demanding but economical high-voltage alternating current system.
Between Paris and Lille new record-breaking passenger trains were introduced, averaging 130km/h (80mph) or more. These successes induced foreign railways to call on French assistance in electrification schemes. By the late 1970s, the earlier types of French electric locomotive were becoming obsolete, and were being replaced by variants like this, No. 6522, with ultra-modern electronic control systems.

Britain was not among the leaders in electrification although an advanced locomotive was built for the North Eastern Railway in 1922. The first major British electrification scheme using the new high-voltage alternating current system was from London to Birmingham, Manchester, and Liverpool (*left*). This was later extended to Glasgow. With electrification, a completely new fast and reliable passenger service was introduced. This attracted many new clients; so many in fact that the investment could be expected to pay for itself within a few years. When the heavily graded line to Glasgow was electrified a new class of more powerful locomotives was needed, and the Class 87 was built to fill this requirement. Having four axles, and weighing only 83 tonnes (81 tons), it was capable of exerting 5,000hp for one hour (that is, before the traction motors overheated). In wet weather, however, the low weight is a disadvantage. Full power cannot be applied because of wheel-slip. As a result, the expected ability to take 914 tonnes (900 tons) trains over Beattock Summit was not obtained, and two locomotives are used for trains of over 609 tonnes (600 tons).

Below is one of the Austrian State Railways' older locomotives, built in Vienna in 1928.

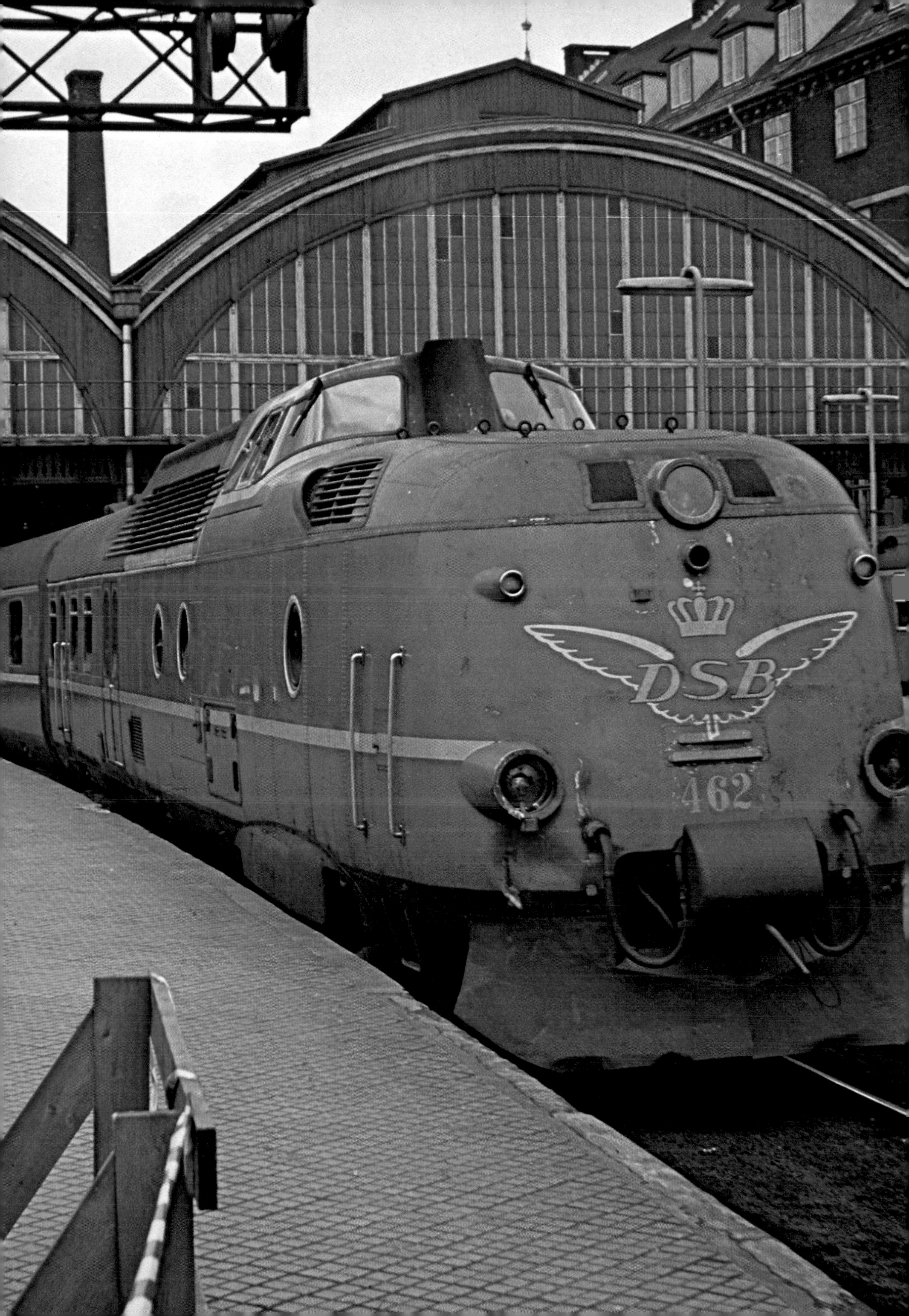
DSB
462

A precursor of the present-day British High Speed Train, was the *Lyntog* diesel multiple unit train of the Danish State Railways (*far left*). This was not especially fast by modern standards, but it provided Denmark with useful, frequent, and reliable passenger services. Because Denmark is divided by so many wide water barriers, punctual operation was essential, since in that country trains had to catch ferries. The length of these trains was limited so that they could be accommodated on the boat decks. Although the current replacements for these trains are diesel-hauled, it is expected that the Danish main lines will be electrified over the next decade.

The Rhaetian Railway in Switzerland is independent and of metre gauge, but it operates trains which are quite as good as those of the standard-gauge Swiss Federal Railways. Above is one of them, shown in characteristic mountainous terrain.

Left is an electric multiple unit train of the Spanish State Railways (RENFE).

North America

It was in America that the diesel-electric locomotive first proved itself as a commercial proposition (as a technical proposition it was proved in Europe around 1914). Since the late 1930s, when General Motors convinced the majority of US railroad managements that the diesel locomotive could reduce costs and improve services, the American diesel locomotive has developed rapidly, especially in the direction of higher horsepower per unit. Several generations of diesel locomotive design are shown in this line-up (*top right*) of modern motive power at a locomotive depot of the Southern Pacific Railroad. On the left, for example, No. 1194 is a yard locomotive very little different from the switching locomotives bought by US railroads in the 1930s. It was yard work for which diesel traction seemed most suitable in the 1930s, because steam locomotives were especially inefficient at this work, having to return to their depot for fuelling and attention after eight hours or so. A diesel locomotive could stay on duty for days on end. Next from the left is a road-switcher, a type which appeared on the eve of World War II and was originally known as a GP (general purpose). Locomotives of this configuration became very popular, and later versions, which can be seen in the centre and extreme right, have the low-nose profile, which gives improved visibility. The centre locomotive is carrying a special livery in honour of the Bi-Centenary of 1976. Second from the right, in the rear, is a passenger locomotive of the Amtrak Corporation. This is the most modern of the US diesel passenger locomotive designs. It was built after a long interval in which the US railroads did not order any new passenger units, because of the dismal prospects for passenger traffic. Partly because of this interval, US manufacturers fell behind in the passenger field, and several overseas companies have shown interest in entering the US market.

The outline of the traditional General Motors diesel locomotive (*right*) is now disappearing. This pair of units belongs to the Canadian Pacific Railway.

Two of the modern generation of passenger diesel locomotives head Amtrak's 'Coast Starlight' out of Seattle (*far right*).

3197
SPIRIT of '76
SP
Amtrak

Australia

High-speed trains have been promised for New South Wales in the next few years. In the meantime, Australia's nearest approach to the concept is the fast connection provided by *The Prospector* service from Kalgoorlie westwards across Western Australia to Perth (*right*). With the regauging of many Western Australian Government Railways' main lines and the introduction of the transcontinental 'Indian Pacific' passenger service, there was an opportunity in the late 1960s to recast passenger services, and *The Prospector* was one result of this. The train is built by Commonwealth Engineering, an Australian company that also built the rolling stock for the 'Indian Pacific' service. For the proposed high speed inter-city services in New South Wales, this company is hoping to supply either 25 multiple unit trains similar to *The Prospector*, or a true HST based on the British High Speed Train. However, due to the state of the track, speeds of 110–130km/h (70–80mph) would be the limit for both services. With most of its population living in big cities, Australia possesses two of the world's busiest railway commuter systems at Sydney and Melbourne. These have been electrified since the early 1930s, and have been extended in recent years. The Eastern Suburbs extension at Sydney, in particular, has transformed the life of one of that city's residential districts. The Sydney system, which combines a dense network in the inner suburbs and long mileages into the country, has been improved in recent years by the introduction of new trains. These make use of doubledeck rolling stock, which carries more passengers without the need to lengthen station platforms. The picture below shows one of the more conventional units used by Victorian Railways for its Melbourne services.

THE
PROSPECTOR

TODAY'S AND TOMORROW'S TRAINS

The British HST (High Speed Train) might be described as tomorrow's train operating today, for it was designed to reach 125mph in daily service on existing track. But there are other ways of creating high-speed services: the gas-turbine train and the Advanced Passenger Train (APT) are now far advanced. Other trains of the future, like those of the new Paris–Sud-Est railway, have not yet entered service, but promise to be equally exciting.

Europe

In 1978, 11 years after the concept was first announced, British Rail unveiled its pre-production Advanced Passenger Train (APT) (*top right*). It was expected that further pre-production trains would enter regular passenger service in 1979, for evaluation. The APT is a high-speed train which can run on existing track even when the latter includes lengths of fairly sharp curves. The individual cars have an automatic tilting arrangement that eases the gravitational forces which the passengers would otherwise feel when passing, at high speed, curves banked only for moderate speeds. The production APTs are expected to have 10 passenger vehicles and one leading, electric-power car. A schedule of 4hr 5min is envisaged between London and Glasgow, compared with the 5 hours that would be required by an HST.
In the late 1960s the possibilities of the gas turbine were studied by several railways (*far right*). The French made the greatest effort, and their turbotrains from Paris to Normandy have been a great commercial success. This picture shows a test train assembled by the German Federal Railways (DB). A retired power car from a TEE train was fitted experimentally with a gas-turbine. However, the high fuel consumption of the gas turbine made the concept less attractive in the 1970s, when oil became much more expensive. The gas turbine accordingly was not adopted by the German Federal Railways, and even in France its further development may be held back.
By 1983 the French Railways (SNCF) will be operating the world's fastest trains between Paris and Lyons over the Paris–Sud-Est Railway. The latter, under construction, is a railway designed specially for very high speeds, and the TGV (*trés grand vitesse*) (*right*) trains will reach 260km/h (162mph). These trains will be electric, and able to run freely over the older, conventional lines. To obtain experience of such high speeds the SNCF built the TGV-001, illustrated here. This turbine-powered train, its work done, was withdrawn in 1979 after having run 15,000 miles at speeds up to 318.6km/h (198mph). The production trains for the Paris–Sud-Est Railway will be very similar, but electrically powered.

INTER
CITY

SNCF

Amtrak

VIA

North America

Before the national VIA organization took over responsibility for the passenger services of the two major Canadian railways, the Canadian National Railways had introduced several innovations to attract passengers from the airlines and highways. Among these were the fast turbotrains built by United Aircraft. These seven-car trains did provide a fast and attractive service between Montreal and Toronto, but they suffered frequent breakdowns and had to be temporarily withdrawn from service. They were then remodelled by the manufacturers and returned to the CNR, subsequently joining the VIA fleet (*below left*). They are now nine-car sets, with each set having five aircraft-type gas turbines of 520hp each (four being used for traction and one to provide heating and lighting power). These engines can be changed in two hours. The trains re-entered service in 1973 and brought the Toronto–Montreal schedule down to 4hr 10min for the 539km (335m), including two suburban stops. This represented an average speed of 129km/h (80mph); top speed of the trains is 154.5km/h (96mph). A special guidance mechanism, and a suspension which includes a tilting arrangement, makes the high speed tolerable over curved track. The trains provide 372 seats, of which 110 are in 'Turboclub' parlour cars. Two dome cars are fitted out as lounges; one such dome, part of the leading power car, can be seen in the picture. These trains are proving an attractive proposition and have drawn many inter-city passengers from their automobiles.

In the 1960s, as more and more passengers deserted the railroads, the USA fell behind other nations in the design and operation of fast passenger trains. When it was decided to catch up the lost ground, one innovation was the acquisition of gas turbine trains from both American and French builders. Three United Aircraft trains were used in a Boston–New York service, and two French trains were bought for trial between Chicago and St Louis. The latter proved so popular and reliable that further sets were bought from France and from the Rohr Corporation (which built the French design under licence). One of the French design trains is pictured here (*top left*) at Montreal.

とき
TOKI

Japan

The Japanese National Railways' New Tokaido Line (*top and above*) between Tokyo and Osaka quite justifiably attracted world attention in the mid-1960s. This was not only because the trains could reach a maximum speed of 257km/h (160 mph) and normally cruised at 209km/h (130mph), but also because the line had been built as a completely new railway, reserved for fast passenger traffic. Freight and slow passenger trains were routed over the older railway. Moreover, the standard gauge was used, not the 1067mm (3ft 6in) gauge of existing lines. Eventually it was intended to create a basic inter-city network of these new lines, and this ambition has to some extent now been achieved. However, progress in this has been slower than expected.

The electric multiple unit (*left*) is very much favoured in Japan, being very suited to the moderate distances and intensive service.

INDEX

Italicized numbers refer to illustrations

Introduction by Christopher Pick

First published in 1979 by
Galley Press in association with
Cathay Books
59 Grosvenor Street, London W1

ISBN 0 86178 011 6

Produced by
Mandarin Publishers Limited
22a Westlands Road
Quarry Bay, Hong Kong

Printed in Singapore.

PDO 79-151

ACME
MILWAUKEE ROAD
MILWAUKEE ROAD
ERIE LACKAWANNA
MILWAUKEE ROAD
ERIE LACKAWANNA
N&W
NORFOLK AND WESTERN
BAR
PITTSBURGH & LAKE ERIE
CHICAGO & EASTERN ILLINOIS
ILLINOIS CENTRAL
Main Line of MID-AMERICA
UNION PACIFIC RAILROAD
automated rail way